# GREAT AFRICAN AMERICANS IN

# FILM

## JANICE PARKER

### Crabtree Publishing Company

# Dedication

This series is dedicated to the African-American men and women who followed their dreams. With courage, faith, and hard work, they overcame obstacles in their lives and went on to excel in their fields. They set standards as some of the best Olympic athletes in the world. They brought innovation to film, jazz, and the arts, and the world is richer for their touch. They became leaders, and through their example encouraged hope and self-reliance. *Outstanding African Americans* is both an acknowledgment of and a tribute to these people.

**Project Manager**
Lauri Seidlitz

**Production Manager**
Amanda Howard

**Editor**
Virginia Mainprize

**Copy Editor**
Janice Parker

**Design**
Warren Clark

**Layout**
Chris Bowerman

**Photograph Credits**
**Cover:** Freeman photo (Photofest), Tyson photo (Globe Photos), Washington photo (Reuters/Bettmann); **Archive Photos:** pages 32 (Joel Levinson), 25, 52; **Globe Photos:** pages 10, 30 (Michael Ferguson), 15, 45 (Fitzroy Barrett), 26 (Milan Ryba), 34 (Rose Hartman), 35 (Ralph Dominguez), 37 (Richard Felber), 55 (Tom Rodriguez), 4, 6, 20, 22, 23, 28; **Photofest:** pages 5, 8, 13, 14, 18, 24, 31, 36, 38, 39, 40, 42, 46, 58, 61; **Reuters/Corbis-Bettmann:** pages 29 (Lee Celano), 33 (Fred Prouser), 43; **Rogers & Cowan:** page 44 (Alastair Thain); **Schomburg Center for Research in Black Culture, New York Public Library:** pages 11, 49; **UPI/Corbis-Bettmann:** pages 7 (Barney Coons), 27 (Sam Mircovich), 9, 19, 21; **Urban Archives, Temple University, Philadelphia, Pennsylvania:** pages 12 (Warners Brothers Records), 17 (CBS Photo), 41 (Avco Embassy Pictures), 16.

Every reasonable effort has been made to trace ownership and to obtain permission to reprint copyright material. The publishers would be pleased to have any errors or omissions brought to their attention so that they may be corrected in subsequent printings.

Published by
Crabtree Publishing Company

| 350 Fifth Avenue, | 360 York Road, R.R. 4 | 73 Lime Walk |
|---|---|---|
| Suite 3308 | Niagara-on-the-Lake | Headington |
| New York, NY | Ontario, Canada | Oxford OX3 7AD |
| U.S.A. 10018 | L0S 1J0 | United Kingdom |

Cataloging-in-Publication Data

Parker, Janice.
    Great African Americans in film / Janice Parker.
      p.  cm. — (Outstanding African Americans)
    Includes index.
    Summary: Contains thirteen biographies of African-American movie stars, including Dorothy Dandridge, Morgan Freeman, Richard Pryor, and Butterfly McQueen.
    ISBN 0-86505-822-9 (pbk.). — ISBN 0-86505-808-3 (RLB)
    1. Afro-American motion picture actors and actresses —Biography—Juvenile literature.  [1. Actors and actresses. 2. Afro-Americans—Biography.]  I. Title.  II. Series.
PN1998.2.P37  1997
791.43'028'092273—dc21
[B]                         96-46677
                                       CIP
                                       AC

# Contents

*For other great African Americans in film, see the book*

**GREAT AFRICAN AMERICANS IN ENTERTAINMENT**
Whoopie Goldberg • Spike Lee • Sidney Poitier • James Earl Jones...and others!

# Dorothy Dandridge

## Personality Profile

**Career:** Actor.

**Born:** November 9, 1922, in Cleveland, Ohio, to Cyril and Ruby Dandridge.

**Died:** September 8, 1965, in Los Angeles, California.

**Family:** Married Harold Nicholas, 1943, (divorced); married Jack Dennison, 1959. Had one daughter, Harolyn.

**Awards:** Nominated for best actress Academy Award for *Carmen Jones*, 1954; nominated for Foreign Press Golden Globe Award for best actress in a musical for *Porgy and Bess*, 1959.

# Growing Up

**D**orothy Dandridge began performing as a young girl. As children, Dorothy and her older sister Vivian starred in an act called The Wonder Kids, singing and dancing at schools and churches. Dorothy's mother wanted to become an actor, so she left her husband and took her two girls to Los Angeles, California, hoping to find work in Hollywood.

In 1937, when Dorothy was fifteen years old, she, her sister, and another girl formed a singing group called The Dandridge Sisters and toured the country with a popular band. They were a hit. They beat twenty-five other acts to win first place in an amateur competition put on by a Los Angeles radio station.

While they were still teenagers, The Dandridge Sisters performed at the Cotton Club, a famous nightclub in New York City that featured African-American performers and famous jazz musicians. The Dandridge Sisters were so popular that they were given a regular spot on the program.

*"I consider myself an actress, and I have always worked to be a confident one."*

Dorothy's group also began to appear in Hollywood movies. In 1937, they got a small part in a Marx Brothers film, *A Day at the Races*. Two years later, they appeared with jazz musician Louis Armstrong in the movie *Going Places*.

# Developing Skills

When Dorothy began her acting career, it was very unusual for a black woman to become a successful film actor. But Dorothy was determined to succeed. She studied acting, dancing, and singing. After a few years, all of Dorothy's hard work paid off when she became one of the first African-American women to get leading roles in films. In 1951, she appeared as an African princess in *Tarzan's Peril*. In 1953, Dorothy had a role as a teacher in the film *Bright Road*.

*Dorothy could act, dance, and sing.*

Dorothy's big break came in the 1954 film *Carmen Jones*. Based on an opera, *Carmen Jones* is the tragic story of a young, black woman in the South. The film was a huge success, and Dorothy was nominated for an Academy Award for her role. It was the first time that an African American was nominated for best actor or actress award.

Her role in *Carmen Jones* brought Dorothy the success she had dreamed of all her life. Stories about her were featured in both the black and white press. In 1954, she became the first African-American woman on the cover of *Life* magazine, which called her one of the most beautiful women in America. She was constantly followed by reporters and photographers.

Dorothy continued to act in several other films, including *Island in the Sun*. This was the first major American film to have an African-American woman in a lead role opposite a white male. Some people were shocked to see a black woman and white man together in a screen romance. Many theaters, particularly those in the South, refused to show the film. A law was almost passed in South Carolina that would have fined movie theaters where the film was shown.

Dorothy's last important film role was in the 1959 all-black musical *Porgy and Bess*. For this part, she was nominated for a Foreign Press Golden Globe Award for best actress in a musical.

*Dorothy arriving for the premiere of* **Carmen Jones** *in New York City.*

## Accomplishments

| | |
|---|---|
| **1937** | Appeared in *A Day at the Races*. |
| **1939** | Appeared with The Dandridge Sisters in *Going Places*. |
| **1954** | Starred in *Carmen Jones*. Nominated for an Academy Award for best actress. Became first African-American woman to appear on the cover of *Life* magazine. |

| | |
|---|---|
| **1957** | Starred in *Island in the Sun* |
| **1959** | Appeared in *Porgy and Bess*. Nominated for a Foreign Press Golden Globe Award for best actress in a musical. |

# Overcoming Obstacles

"My sister worked twenty-four hours a day at being a star."
— Vivian Dandridge.

After her success with The Dandridge Sisters act, Dorothy decided to put her career on hold. She got married, settled down, and had a daughter, Harolyn. Soon, she discovered that her daughter had been born severely brain damaged. Dorothy went from doctor to doctor hoping something could be done. Sadly, Harolyn had to be put in hospital for the rest of her life. Soon after that, Dorothy's marriage ended in divorce. She was so shattered that she decided to devote herself fully to her career.

Dorothy was very shy and often got extremely nervous about performing. At her opening night at a Los Angeles club, she was so nervous that she had to sit down to do her act. Her manager had to work with her before each performance to build up her confidence. Dorothy began to relax. People loved the show, and her next night club act at the Mocambo broke all attendance records.

*At first, Dorothy was turned down for* **Carmen Jones** *because the director thought she was too classy.*

Despite being shy, Dorothy was also a fighter. When she first auditioned for *Carmen Jones*, she was turned down for the lead. The director said she was too classy for the part. Dorothy changed the way she dressed and moved, and she taught herself how to speak with a southern accent. When she returned to audition again, the director was so impressed that he gave her the role.

Racism limited Dorothy's film career. Audiences could not accept an African-American woman in major film roles. Even after Dorothy became famous, she was often forced to work in nightclubs to earn a living. She was not offered as many film roles as she had hoped for, and most of them were very similar—a dark-skinned woman who was doomed to live in sadness.

The parts that Dorothy played often mirrored her real life. She had many tragic relationships with white men. Her second marriage to a white restaurant owner was a disaster. Dorothy poured her savings into her husband's business and lost all her money. Then he left her.

*In 1963, Dorothy had to declare bankruptcy.*

Alone, with no money and no film offers, Dorothy began to take pills for her depression. She drank heavily and her health was poor. Then things seemed to improve. Dorothy traveled to Mexico, went to a health spa, and signed a contract for a new movie. A few days after her return to Hollywood, she was found dead in her apartment from an overdose of pills. She was forty-two years old.

## Special Interests

- Dorothy was very thrifty. Until her second marriage, she saved most of the money she made from films.
- Dorothy put all her energy into her work. She exercised daily, improved her voice, and bought beautiful costumes.

# Morgan Freeman

## Personality Profile

**Career:** Actor.

**Born:** June 1, 1937, in Memphis, Tennessee, to Morgan and Mayme Freeman.

**Education:** Los Angeles City College.

**Family:** Married Jeanette Adair Bradshaw, 1967, (divorced, 1979); married Myrna Colley-Lee, 1984. Has two sons, Alphonso and Saifoulaye, and two daughters, Deena and Morgana.

**Awards:** Obie award for the stage version of *Driving Miss Daisy*, 1987; New York Film Critics Circle Award, Los Angeles Film Critics Award, National Society of Film Critics Award for *Street Smart*, 1987; Golden Globe Award and Academy Award nomination for the film version of *Driving Miss Daisy*, 1989; Academy Award best actor nomination for *The Shawshank Redemption*, 1995.

# Growing Up

Because Morgan's childhood was so difficult, he prefers not to talk about it in interviews. In 1939, when Morgan was two, he was sent to live with his grandmother in Mississippi. When she died, four years later, he went to live with his parents in Chicago. Morgan arrived in the middle of winter, and was shocked at the cold. He was used to the warm humidity of the South. After six months, Morgan's mother left her husband and took Morgan back to Greenwood, Mississippi. They did not stay for long, and Morgan remembers moving from place to place during most of his childhood.

Morgan acted for the first time when he was eight years old. He played the lead in a school play, *Little Boy Blue.* As a teenager, Morgan was encouraged to act in school plays so he would keep out of trouble. Once, he pulled a chair out from under a girl he liked in his class. Instead of punishing him, his teacher offered Morgan a part in the school play. For that role, he won a state championship prize for best actor.

Even though Morgan showed such early talent, he did not take acting seriously. After high school, he was offered a partial scholarship to study theater in Jackson, Mississippi. But Morgan turned down this opportunity and joined the U.S. Air Force in 1955.

*One of Morgan's earliest jobs was on a children's educational television series.*

*"I've been offered black quasi-heroes who get hanged at the end. I won't do a part like that. If I do a hero, he's going to live to the end of the movie."*

# Developing Skills

Morgan left the air force after a few years. He thought that his acting talent would make it easy for him to get theater work. He was wrong. To support himself, he worked at various jobs, such as a clerk, a car washer, and a dancer at the 1964 World's Fair. During this time, he also studied dance and attended acting school.

In the late 1960s, Morgan got some good theater roles. He made his film debut in 1971, playing a character named Afro in *Who Says I Can't Ride a Rainbow*!

*As "The Electric Company's" far-out disc jockey, Morgan made reading cool.*

That same year, Morgan also began working on the children's television series "The Electric Company." He played a cool disc jockey, named Easy Reader, who talked about the importance of reading. He enjoyed the steady work but did not feel challenged as an actor. He left the show in 1976.

Soon, Morgan was getting lead roles in both plays and movies. *New Yorker* magazine called him "the greatest actor in America." In 1987, he received an Academy Award nomination for his part in the film *Street Smart* in which he played a tough criminal.

In 1989, Morgan played the part of Hoke, the chauffeur of a wealthy, white woman, in the movie *Driving Miss Daisy*. He had played the same role on stage in 1987. Once again, critics and audiences were impressed by his acting talents. He was nominated for another Academy Award.

Later that year, Morgan was in *Glory*, a film about an all-black army unit during the Civil War. Morgan considers his work in *Glory* to be one of his most satisfying parts. He described the movie as "a moment in history that has been...forgotten about. To bring it back where it belongs, close to the heart, is a wonderful undertaking."

Since then, Morgan's career has soared. He is known as a character actor who can play completely different roles with the same skill. He has starred in a number of movies, but Morgan is not interested in stardom. All he wishes for is "steady work."

*Morgan received an Academy Award nomination for his role in* **Driving Miss Daisy.**

## Accomplishments

**1967** Appeared on stage in *Hello Dolly*.

**1971-76** Played the part of Easy Reader on "The Electric Company."

**1978** Won a Drama Desk Award and a Tony nomination for his role in the play *The Mighty Gents*.

**1987** Appeared in the stage version of *Driving Miss Daisy*. Won a Golden Globe Award for his role in the film *Street Smart*.

**1989** Appeared in a film version of *Driving Miss Daisy* and *Glory*.

**1991** Acted in *Robin Hood: Prince of Thieves*.

**1992** Starred with Clint Eastwood in the western film *Unforgiven*.

**1993** Directed his first film, *Bopha!*

**1995** Costarred with Brad Pitt in *Seven* and with Tim Robbins in *The Shawshank Redemption*. Nominated for best actor Academy Award for *The Shawshank Redemption*.

# Overcoming Obstacles

*Morgan in* **The Shawshank Redemption.**

When he was growing up, Morgan had many hard times. Moving around so often was difficult. All he remembers about his time in Chicago is moving from one dark, tiny apartment to another. About those years, Morgan says that "the windowsills were our freezer, and once we lived in a building that stood by itself on an empty lot."

As a teenager, Morgan got involved with a street gang called The Spiders and started stealing. But he was very bright and excelled in school. Morgan always went to his classes because school helped him forget about his problems. Films were another escape for him. He collected bottles to get enough money to pay for movie tickets. Like school, going to see movies helped keep him out of trouble.

Morgan loved war movies and hoped to become a fighter pilot when he joined the air force. Tests showed he had the ability, but because he was black, he was made a radar mechanic instead. The air force was not prepared to give Morgan the important job of pilot.

Early in his career, Morgan was unable to get the kinds of roles he wanted. He began to drink. One night, he passed out on his doorstep after drinking too much. He decided to quit drinking.

Despite his reputation as a talented actor, Morgan often had difficulty finding good roles. In 1982, Morgan auditioned for a part in Paul Newman's film *Harry and Son*. Morgan did not get the part, but Paul was shocked that an actor as talented as Morgan had not been able to find work for two years. Paul gave Morgan another role in the movie.

Morgan is critical of many of the film roles offered to African Americans. He refuses many parts and only chooses those that will best develop his career as an actor. In 1993, he made his own opportunity. He directed the movie *Bopha* and became one of the few African Americans to direct a major film.

*Morgan with his wife Myrna.*

## Special Interests

- Morgan loves sailing and sometimes goes on trips that last for several months on his sailboat, *The Sojourner*. He plans to sail around the world someday.

# Hattie McDaniel

## Personality Profile

**Career:** Actor and singer.

**Born:** June 10, 1895, in Wichita, Kansas, to Henry and Susan McDaniel.

**Died:** October 26, 1952, in Woodland Hills, California.

**Education:** Dropped out of high school after her sophomore year.

**Family:** Married George Langford, 1922, (died); married Howard Hickman, (divorced, 1938); married James Lloyd Crawford, 1941, (divorced); married Larry Williams, 1949, (divorced).

**Awards:** Academy Award for best supporting actress in *Gone with the Wind*, 1940; inducted into Black Filmmakers Hall of Fame, 1975.

# Growing Up

**H**attie McDaniel grew up in a very talented family. Her father, who had been a slave on a Virginia plantation, was a Baptist minister, singer, dancer, guitar and banjo player. Hattie's mother sang in a gospel group. Some of Hattie's twelve brothers and sisters had successful careers as singers and actors.

Hattie's parents moved to Denver, Colorado, soon after Hattie was born. Although she was one of only a few black students in elementary school, Hattie was treated the same as everybody else. All of her teachers and classmates loved the outspoken and energetic, young girl.

Even at a young age, Hattie was comfortable being the center of attention. She sang at church and liked to recite poetry and passages from the Bible for her classmates. She performed in school plays and musicals, and she loved to dance.

*"I portray the type of Negro woman who has worked honestly and proudly."*

In 1910, at the age of fifteen, Hattie won a gold medal for dramatic art. She recited the poem "Convict Joe," and many members of the audience were moved to tears by her performance. Hattie got a standing ovation for her recital.

Although Hattie was a good student, she quit high school. She felt that it was time for her performing career to begin.

# Developing Skills

H attie began her career as a singer, not an actor. In her teens, she joined her brother Otis's touring group of entertainers. They traveled from town to town, putting on their shows in tents. Hattie wrote and performed many of their songs. In 1915, she sang on a Denver radio station and became the first African-American woman to sing on the radio.

*Hattie in* **Gone with the Wind.**

During the following years, Hattie sang with other groups. She joined the touring company of the musical *Showboat* in 1925. A few years later, finding herself out of work, she got a job as a maid in a hotel in Milwaukee, Wisconsin. She did not stay a maid for long. She auditioned for the hotel's variety show and won a starring role.

Hattie moved to Hollywood. She appeared in dozens of movies before she got the role she is best known for in *Gone with the Wind.* Hattie's friends encouraged her to try out for the part of Mammy, the family maid. The role was perfectly suited to the lively, bossy Hattie. She read the book on which the film was based three times to prepare for her audition. When she went for her screen test, she dressed the part of a southern mammy. After one look at Hattie, the producer of the movie canceled all other auditions. He knew that he had found his Mammy.

*"It's better to get seven thousand dollars a week for playing a servant than seven dollars a week for being one."*

*Gone with the Wind* became one of the most popular films of all time. On February 29, 1940, Hattie became the first African American ever to win an Oscar. At the Academy Awards ceremony, she received two standing ovations.

Hattie acted in over 300 other movies. In 1947, she returned to radio, starring in the comedy series "Beulah." The show became a hit, and Hattie received hundreds of letters a day from her fans across the country. Her salary was two thousand dollars a week, and her contract allowed her to change any script. Hattie was about to play the part of Beulah on a television series when she died of cancer in 1952. Her funeral was attended by her many friends in the movie business and thousands of her loyal fans.

*Hattie won an Oscar for her role as Mammy in* **Gone with the Wind.**

## Accomplishments

**1910** Won gold medal for recital of poem "Convict Joe."

**1925** First radio appearance.

**1932** Acted in first movie, *The Golden West.*

**1940** Was the first African American to win an Academy Award for best supporting actress in *Gone with the Wind.*

**1947** Starred on radio in "Beulah."

**1975** Inducted into the Black Filmmakers Hall of Fame.

# Overcoming Obstacles

Hattie's success was as much due to her hard work and determination as to her talents. During her career, Hattie appeared in more than 300 movies. However, she received credit for only about seventy of them. Her roles were often overlooked even though she could steal the show from better-known actors. She could never completely support herself from her film acting and often took radio jobs or worked as a maid.

*Hattie in 1948 on the set of "Beulah."*

On film and radio, Hattie played the parts of maids. Hattie's maids were not quiet servants in the background. Her strong personality and wonderful voice turned them into characters who were wiser than the white people they served.

In the 1940s, the National Association for the Advancement of Colored People (NAACP) criticized Hattie for always taking the roles of servants. The NAACP put pressure on black actors to accept only acting parts that would show African-American people in a positive way. Hattie was accused of hurting the image of African Americans.

The NAACP's actions upset and angered Hattie. Although she was proud of being African American, she was also proud of her work in films. She was also realistic. She knew there were few opportunities for black actors, and that there was little chance for her to play other types of characters. Racism was strong in those days. Even when Hattie attended the Academy Award ceremonies, she was seated at the back of the room.

Hattie fought racism in her own way. She helped organize entertainment for the black troops in World War II, and she raised money for educational scholarships for young African Americans.

*Hattie liked to collect figurines and was proud of her home in Los Angeles.*

In 1945, Hattie went to court to keep her house in a white neighborhood in Los Angeles. Her neighbors had tried to prevent Hattie and other African Americans from buying houses in the area. Hattie took the case to the Superior Court and won. Her efforts helped change the law for equal housing practices in the United States.

## Special Interests

- Hattie loved to get fan mail and often wrote back to her fans.
- She was very soft-hearted and helped people who needed money.

# Richard Pryor

## Personality Profile

**Career:** Actor, writer, and comedian.

**Born:** December 1, 1940, in Peoria, Illinois, to LeRoy and Gertrude Pryor.

**Education:** Expelled from high school.

**Family:** Married and divorced five times. Has seven children: Renee, Richard Jr., Rain, Elizabeth, Steven, Kelsey, and Franklin.

**Awards:** Emmy award for "Lily," 1973; Writers Guild award and American Academy of Humor award for *Blazing Saddles,* 1974; Grammy awards for Best Comedy Recording, 1974, 1975, 1976, 1981, 1982.

# Growing Up

**L**ife has not often been easy for Richard. His parents were not married. His mother worked as a prostitute and often disappeared for months at a time. When Richard was ten, she walked out for good. Richard had little contact with his father and was raised by his grandmother who beat him when he did not behave. He was often in trouble with the police.

*"I was a skinny little black kid with big eyes that took in the whole world and a wide smile that begged for more attention than anybody had time to give."*

One day, Richard discovered he could make people laugh. He fell off the porch railing on purpose and everyone roared. Richard realized this was the best way to get people's attention and approval.

When Richard was eleven years old, a teacher encouraged him to act in a community play. She also let him stand in front of the class and entertain his classmates. He performed skits that the other kids loved. One of his stories was about the Rummage Sale Ranger, a black superhero who cannot afford to buy superhero clothes and searches rummage sales for his cape and shoes. The teacher's support was very important to Richard. When he won an Emmy in 1973, he gave the award to the elementary school teacher who had encouraged him.

Richard continued to have problems in school. He was expelled from grade eight for swinging a punch at his science teacher. He never returned to school.

# Developing Skills

After serving in the army for two years, Richard began to work as a comedian. He started as a stand-up comic in a black comedy club in Peoria, Illinois. Within a few years, he was performing in other nearby cities. Finally, he was being paid for doing what he loved—entertaining people.

In 1963, Richard moved to New York City. He appeared on two popular television shows, the "Ed Sullivan Show" and the "Merv Griffin Show." Richard's routines were sometimes shockingly honest about life as an African American. Richard had developed a new way of performing—he turned personal and sometimes painful events from his own life into comedy.

**Richard in Live on the Sunset Strip.**

After moving to Los Angeles, Richard began to get small parts in movies. He was nominated for an Academy Award for his supporting role in a film about jazz singer Billie Holiday in *Lady Sings the Blues*.

Richard's comedy skills improved, and he wrote for several popular television series, such as "The Flip Wilson Show" and "Sanford and Son." He also helped Mel Brooks write the screenplay for *Blazing Saddles*, a successful comedy-Western. In 1973, Richard won an Emmy award for a television special, "Lily," starring Lily Tomlin. In 1979, Richard released a film of his comedy act called *Richard Pryor Live in Concert*. Many people consider this film to contain some of his best work.

In 1985, Richard wrote, directed, and starred in *Jo Jo Dancer, Your Life Is Calling*. The film was partly based on Richard's own life and was his first chance to direct. Richard knew from experience how hard it was for African Americans to get jobs in the film industry, so he hired only African Americans for the movie.

Richard was diagnosed with multiple sclerosis in 1986. Three years later, he co-starred with Eddie Murphy in the movie *Harlem Nights*. He looked thin and frail, and soon he was too weak to work on films.

In 1995, Richard published an autobiography called *Pryor Convictions and Other Life Sentences*. He has been a major influence on many of today's young comedians and actors. His ability to turn obstacles into success can inspire all Americans.

***Richard with Gene Wilder in* Stir Crazy.**

## Accomplishments

| | |
|---|---|
| **1964** Appeared for the first time on television in "Broadway Tonight." | **1981-82** Won Grammy awards for Best Comedy Recording. |
| **1972** Nominated for an Academy Award for best supporting actor in *Lady Sings the Blues*. | **1985** Wrote, directed, and starred in *Jo Jo Dancer, Your Life Is Calling*. |
| **1973** Won an Emmy award for "Lily." | **1989** Appeared with Eddie Murphy in *Harlem Nights*. |
| **1974-76** Won Grammy awards for Best Comedy Recording. | **1995** Released autobiography, *Pryor Convictions and Other Life Sentences*. |
| **1979** Released *Richard Pryor Live in Concert*. | |

# Overcoming Obstacles

R ichard's childhood was very difficult. He was surrounded by prostitutes and criminals. He was physically and sexually abused. Despite this, he does not feel anger or bitterness. He feels thankful for all of the good things that have happened to him.

One of the reasons that audiences like Richard is because he talks about problems that many people face. They understand what he is talking about because he has experienced so many problems himself. Richard has the talent to make people laugh about the sad events in their lives. Comedian Bill Cosby has said that "for Richard, the line between comedy and tragedy is as fine as you can paint it."

Richard was often criticized for the crude language he used in his routines. Many people were shocked, but Richard's up-front approach opened the door for later comedians who followed in the same comedy style.

Despite his success as a comic and actor, Richard had problems throughout his life. He has been married and divorced five times. He has abused drugs throughout most of his life. This harmed his health and sometimes made him behave violently. He almost died in 1980 when he set himself on fire while using cocaine.

*Even though Richard must spend most of his time in a wheelchair, he still finds time to socialize. He is pictured here with Jennifer Lee and Byron Allen.*

In 1982, Richard tried to get over his drug problems. He joined a rehabilitation program and worked with other drug abusers to cure his addictions.

Just as he was cleaning up his life, however, he was told he had multiple sclerosis. Multiple sclerosis, or MS, affects the nerves of a person's body. People with MS can end up confined to a wheelchair, unable to walk.

Richard stopped performing in 1992 and now spends much of his time in a wheelchair. He has not let MS stop him from working. He still writes comedy material and has talked about working on a project with African-American director John Singleton.

*Richard received his star on the Hollywood Walk of Fame in 1993.*

## Special Interests

- In the 1970s, Richard became interested in black history. In 1979, he went to Africa. His trip made him realize that people are all the same, whether they are black or white.

# John Singleton

## Personality Profile

**Career:** Screenwriter and director.

**Born:** January 6, 1968, in Los Angeles, California, to Danny Singleton and Sheila Ward-Johnson.

**Education:** University of Southern California School of Cinema-Television, 1990.

**Awards:** Three writing awards at USC. Nominated for two Academy Awards for *Boyz N the Hood*, 1992.

# Growing Up

John was shuffled back and forth between his unmarried parents throughout his childhood. His mother and father were both teenagers when John was born, but both cared very much for their son. John sometimes stole candy and toys, but he did not get into serious trouble. He believes this was because his parents gave him so much attention and support.

When John was a child, his father often took him to the movies. By the time he was nine, John had seen the films of many of the greatest directors, including Orson Welles, Akira Kurosawa, and Steven Spielberg. At this young age, John realized that there were not many films made by or about African Americans. He decided that he wanted to make films about the problems young black people face.

In high school, John discovered that the screenplay or script was one of the most important parts of a film. He decided to become a screenplay writer. After graduating from high school in 1986, John won a scholarship to study film writing at the University of Southern California's School of Cinema-Television. During his four years at college, he won three writing awards.

*"Film has the power to shape, change, and educate."*

# Developing Skills

While still in college, John began his film career with a business-like attitude. He hired an agent who sent his screenplay *Boyz N the Hood* to Columbia Pictures, one of the most important motion picture studios. Columbia was impressed by the script. They agreed to produce John's film but wanted a more experienced person to direct it. John refused, saying that a play about black youths in Los Angeles had to be directed by someone who had lived there. He wanted to control his own film. Columbia finally gave in and gave John $7 million to make his movie.

*Boyz N the Hood* is about young African Americans growing up in the 1990s. The film follows the lives of three teenage boys who live in a tough Los Angeles neighborhood. The main character, Tre, has a strong, caring father. Tre manages to avoid life on the street, become responsible, and enroll in college. Tre's two friends both become victims of the street. The film makes a powerful statement about the importance of African-American fathers in their children's lives.

Many film critics and audiences raved about *Boyz N the Hood*. However, some people criticized the way it showed African-American families. In some large cities, violence broke out near several theaters showing the film, and people were hurt. Despite these problems, many people were impressed by the talents of this young director.

*Besides being the youngest and first African-American director ever nominated for an Academy Award, John has formed his own music video production company.*

*Boyz N the Hood* made more than $100 million. At the age of twenty-three, John became the youngest director and the first African American to be nominated for an Academy Award in the best director category. He has since made two other successful films, *Poetic Justice* and *Higher Learning*. John says he sees himself as the "first filmmaker of the hip-hop generation."

John now has his own company, called New Deal Productions, which produces music videos and soundtracks. He directed Michael Jackson's "Remember the Time" video. John plans to make more films and music videos and would like to make animated movies. He also wants to produce films for other writers and directors and hopes one day to own his own motion picture studio.

*John on the set of* Boyz N the Hood.

## Accomplishments

**1991** Wrote and directed his first film, *Boyz N the Hood*.

**1992** Nominated for two Academy Awards.

**1993** Made *Poetic Justice*, starring Janet Jackson.

**1994** Released his third film, *Higher Learning*.

*"I want to dignify African Americans through films. We need to show them with some dignity. Humanize them, not just with positive images. We need to show a balance of good and bad."*

John has always had confidence in his ideas and his abilities. He has not let his young age stand in his way. When Columbia Pictures did not want him to direct *Boyz N the Hood*, John simply said that he would take his screenplay to another company. He was confident that another studio would give him a chance.

A good part of John's success is the result of his understanding of the business side of the film industry. It is very difficult for inexperienced, young people to get started in movies. By learning about the business aspects of making a motion picture, John was better able to direct his own films.

*Boyz N the Hood* started off with bad publicity. There was violence in and around several theaters that showed the film. Two people died, and thirty were injured. Many theaters refused to show the film, believing the movie was causing violence. John responded, "I didn't create the conditions under which people shoot each other.... This is a generation of kids who don't have father figures. They're looking for their manhood, and they get a gun. The more of those people that get together, the higher the potential for violence."

Many people also criticized John's portrayal of women in the film. John decided to address this problem with his second movie, *Poetic Justice*, which was about African-American women. His second and third films were not as popular as his first, but John was not discouraged. He remained confident of his abilities and was not bothered by criticism. As John said, "I don't feel any pressure from critics. I only feel pressured to make good movies."

John is aware of the problems of racism in America. He believes that young people need to be taught more about African-American history. John thinks that African Americans would feel proud about themselves if they knew more about their past. He is convinced that films can make important social and political statements. He says that "if you make a film, you have a responsibility to say something socially relevant."

*John Singleton and Janet Jackson at the premiere of* **Poetic Justice.**

## Special Interests

- John loves playing with electronic gadgets, including video games and computers.
- He relaxes by reading, watching movies, biking, and scuba diving.

# Cicely Tyson

## Personality Profile

**Career:** Actor.

**Born:** December 19, 1942, in New York City, New York, to William and Theodosia Tyson.

**Education**: Graduated from high school. Studied acting at numerous schools.

**Family:** Married Miles Davis, 1981, (divorced).

**Awards:** Academy Award nomination for best actress in *Sounder*, 1972; Emmy award for role in television drama "The Autobiography of Miss Jane Pittman," 1974; Emmy award for "The Oldest Confederate Widow Tells All," 1994.

# Growing Up

Cicely Tyson grew up as the youngest of three children in Harlem, New York City. Her parents had immigrated from Nevis, a small island in the West Indies before she was born. The Tyson family worked hard, but they found it difficult to make a living. Cicely's father was a carpenter and painter who sometimes had to sell fruit and vegetables to support his family. At the age of nine, Cicely sold shopping bags on the street to make extra money.

Despite her parents' lack of money, Cicely had a positive outlook. She always believed she would one day have a better life. As a child, she often traveled on the bus and subway just to remind herself that there was a world outside her neighborhood.

Cicely's parents separated, and she stayed with her very strict, religious mother. Cicely sang in the church choir and played the piano and organ. She practiced for hours and played the piano so well that she gave concerts in many New York concert halls.

After graduating from high school, Cicely worked at many different jobs. One day, while working as a secretary for the Red Cross, she realized that "God did not put me on this earth to bang on a typewriter for the rest of my life." She quit her job and went to modeling school.

*"When I decided to become an actress I never had any doubt that I would be successful.... My mother had always instilled into us that whatever you try to do, do it as best as you possibly can and if you are good at what you are doing, then success will come to you."*

# Developing Skills

S oon, Cicely became one of the top-ten black models in the United States. In 1956, she was on the cover of both *Vogue* and *Harper's Bazaar* magazines. She got into acting almost by accident. Friends suggested that she audition for a part in a film. Although Cicely was not interested in acting, she went to the audition. Several months later, she was offered the lead in an African-American movie called *The Spectrum*.

*Cicely in **Sounder**, for which she was nominated for an Academy Award.*

After this movie, Cicely decided to study acting seriously. She was offered a role in the motion picture *Twelve Angry Men* in 1957. Two years later, a part in the musical *The Dark Side of the Moon* launched her acting career. In 1963, she got a regular role on the television series "East Side/West Side." She became the first African-American actor to have an on-going part in a dramatic television series.

Cicely continued to work on stage and television and had roles in many films. In 1972, she was offered the part of Rebecca in the movie *Sounder*. Film critics and audiences agreed that she was amazing as the strong, loving woman during the Depression years. Many people said Rebecca was the first positive portrayal of an African American in film. When the National Society of Film Critics gave Cicely an award for the role, she got a five-minute standing ovation.

In 1974, Cicely won an Emmy award for her performance in the television drama "The Autobiography of Miss Jane Pittman." The story was based on the novel by Ernest Gaines, and Cicely played Jane Pittman from the ages of 19 to 110. To prepare for the role, Cicely visited elderly women in a nursing home.

In the 1970s and 1980s, Cicely played a variety of roles, all portraying strong African-American women. These roles included Harriet Tubman, the escaped slave who led three hundred other slaves to freedom, and Coretta Scott King, wife of Martin Luther King, Jr. In 1989, she was in the television movie "The Women of Brewster Place" with Oprah Winfrey. In 1994, Cicely starred in the television series, "Sweet Justice."

*Cicely with Mary Louise Parker in* **Fried Green Tomatoes** *in 1991.*

## Accomplishments

**1957** Appeared in *Twelve Angry Men.*

**1959** Performed first major role on stage in *The Dark Side of the Moon.*

**1963** Regular role in television series "East Side/West Side."

**1972** Starred in *Sounder.* Nominated for an Academy Award for best actress.

**1974** Won Emmy award for "The Autobiography of Miss Jane Pittman."

**1987** Appeared in *Cry Freedom.*

**1989** Appeared in "The Women of Brewster Place."

**1991** Appeared in *Fried Green Tomatoes.*

**1994** Won an Emmy award for "The Oldest Confederate Widow Tells All."

**1994** Starred in the television series "Sweet Justice."

# Overcoming Obstacles

*"I think that life is always striving. I'd like to think that this is just a new beginning and that there are still some untold mysteries out there."*

T he first obstacle to Cicely becoming an actor was her mother. Cicely's mom did not think that acting was a proper job for a young woman. She called Cicely's acting her "foolishness work" and thought that the entertainment industry was sinful. Cicely's mother first saw her daughter act in a play called *The Dark of the Moon* in which Cicely played a prostitute. After the play was over, Cicely's mother went backstage to cover Cicely with her coat. In her acceptance speech after winning her first Emmy award, Cicely said, "You see, Mom, it really wasn't a den of [sin] after all."

Cicely has had difficulty finding enough good acting parts. At times during her career, she has had long periods without work. She believes that this is because she is African American, because she is a woman, and because she is choosy about the roles she takes. In the early part of her career, Cicely was often told that her skin was too dark. Successful African-American actresses at the time had lighter skin and straighter hair. Cicely looked too African for the entertainment industry and was often ignored by the media.

Throughout her career, Cicely has spoken out about the lack of good film roles for African-American women. When Cicely traveled to promote the movie *Sounder*, she realized that "much of America was very ignorant about black people and particularly black women." She decided that she would only accept roles that helped others see what African-American women were really like.

Cicely continues to stand up for what she believes in and to support young actors and performers. Her work has influenced many of today's African-American actors. Cicely helped found the Dance Theater of Harlem to discover and develop the abilities of young performers.

The television series "Sweet Justice" brought Cicely's career full circle. It was the first time she had acted in a regular television series since "East Side/West Side." Her character, a woman who owns a law firm, is a strong person who tries to make the world a better place. In this role, Cicely plays someone who is much like herself—a strong African-American achiever.

*Cicely is very choosy about the roles she will play. In "Sweet Justice" her character is an idealistic lawyer.*

## Special Interests

- Cicely loves to read, go for walks, and cook. She prefers to cook for other people than for herself.
- Cicely enjoys sewing her own clothes.

# Denzel Washington

## Personality Profile

**Career:** Actor.

**Born:** December 28, 1954, in Mount Vernon, New York, to Denzel and Lennis Washington.

**Family:** Married Pauletta Pearson, 1983. Has four children, John David, Katia, and twins Malcolm and Olivia.

**Education:** B.A., Fordham University, 1981.

**Awards:** Obie award for best performance in *A Soldier's Play*, 1981; Academy Award nomination for best supporting actor in *Cry Freedom*, 1989; National Association for the Advancement of Colored People (NAACP) Image Award, 1989; Academy Award for best supporting actor in *Glory*, 1990; Los Angeles Board of Supervisors Martin Luther King, Jr., Award, 1996.

# Growing Up

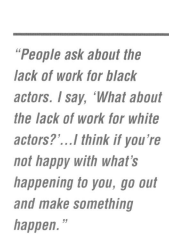

**D**enzel Washington grew up in a middle-class neighborhood on the border of the Bronx in New York City. He had friends from many different backgrounds. Although some of Denzel's childhood friends ended up in prison, he kept out of serious trouble. Denzel believes that his parents' strong support helped him. As he says about his friends, "They were all good guys, but I just had a little more help."

Denzel's father was a minister who allowed his children to watch only animated films or films based on Bible stories. As a child, Denzel had no interest in becoming an actor.

In 1968, when Denzel was fourteen, his parents divorced. Denzel had trouble dealing with his parents' breakup, and he began getting into fights at school. A school counselor believed that a private school might help Denzel. He was a good student, so he applied to an expensive boarding school with mainly wealthy, white students. Much to Denzel's surprise, he was not only accepted into the school, but also he received a full scholarship. In high school, Denzel was not very interested in his studies but was an excellent athlete. He did well in baseball, basketball, football, and track.

After graduating, Denzel went to Fordham University in New York City. At first, he wanted to become a medical doctor and then a journalist. One summer, he took part in a talent show at the YMCA summer camp where he worked. For the first time, he realized that he wanted to become an actor.

*"People ask about the lack of work for black actors. I say, 'What about the lack of work for white actors?'...I think if you're not happy with what's happening to you, go out and make something happen."*

# Developing Skills

It was obvious to everyone that Denzel had natural acting talent. When he returned to school after summer camp, he tried out for the lead in the college play. Although Denzel was studying journalism, he won the part, beating several students who were majoring in theater. Denzel got his first paid acting job in the television movie "Wilma" before he even graduated from university. The movie was about the African-American Olympic champion Wilma Rudolph. After college, Denzel got small parts in films, television shows, and in the theater.

In 1981, Denzel acted in *A Soldier's Play*, a story about racial tensions at an army base during World War II. The production was very successful, and Denzel won an Obie award for his work. The next year, Denzel got a regular part as Dr. Phillip Chandler on the television series "St. Elsewhere." Although it was not his most challenging role, his part in the series made Denzel one of the most popular African-American actors in Hollywood today.

His next important film role was as Steve Biko, the South African black activist in *Cry Freedom*. Over a hundred actors had auditioned for the part of Biko. Although Denzel was pleased to play the part, he was unhappy that the film focused more on a white journalist than on the real hero, Biko himself.

*Denzel starred as civil rights activist Malcolm X in the film* **Malcolm X.**

In 1989, Denzel won an Academy Award for his work in the film *Glory*. He was the fifth African-American actor to win an Oscar. He also won the NAACP Image Award for best supporting actor. Denzel has said that this award was more important to him than his Oscar.

Denzel has always been willing to put extra effort into his acting. For his role in *Cry Freedom*, he gained thirty pounds, had the caps on his front teeth removed, and learned how to speak with a South African accent. For his part as a trumpeter in *Mo' Better Blues*, Denzel spent time with the legendary jazz musician Miles Davis. For his role as Malcolm X, Denzel read Malcolm's books and listened to tapes of him speaking. Denzel wanted the part in *Mississippi Masala* so much that he agreed to work for a quarter of his usual salary.

*Denzel with his Academy Award for best supporting actor in* **Glory**.

## Accomplishments

**1981** Graduated with a B.A. from Fordham University.

**1982-88** Appeared on the television series "St. Elsewhere."

**1984** Appeared in the film *A Soldier's Story*.

**1987** Starred as Steve Biko in *Cry Freedom*.

**1989** Starred in *Glory*. Won an Academy Award and the NAACP Image Award for best supporting actor.

**1990** Starred in Spike Lee's *Mo' Better Blues*.

**1992** Starred as Malcolm X in *Malcolm X*. Starred in *Mississippi Masala*.

**1994** Starred with Sean Connery in *Crimson Tide*.

**1996** Starred in *Courage under Fire* and *The Preacher's Wife*.

# Overcoming Obstacles

**D**espite his talent, confidence, and good looks, Denzel's career has been affected by racism. There are few films made about African Americans, and few African-American actors are offered starring roles in Hollywood movies. Most film critics agree that if Denzel were white, he would have become successful much more quickly. From the beginning of his career, Denzel's roles were limited because of his skin color. Also, he has turned down many parts in films if he did not like how African Americans were portrayed.

As a highly successful actor, Denzel believes that he has a responsibility to portray African Americans in a realistic way. Denzel accepted the part in *Glory* because he believed it was a worthwhile role for an African-American actor. He only agreed to play the role, however, if the screenplay was rewritten to focus more on the black soldiers. Denzel studied about the Civil War and slavery in America. In all of his years in school, he had never been taught about the African Americans who fought in the Civil War. He wanted to make sure that younger generations would know about the proud history of African Americans.

*Denzel is one of the most popular and respected actors in Hollywood today.*

After winning an Oscar in 1990, Denzel was finally considered for leading parts. In 1993, Denzel got two roles that were not specifically written for black actors. In *The Pelican Brief*, he played a journalist, and in *Philadelphia*, he played a lawyer who represents a man with AIDS.

Despite being considered one of the most attractive men in Hollywood, Denzel does not focus on being a movie star. Denzel does not enjoy the Hollywood party scene. His family is the most important thing in the world to him. He thinks of himself first as a husband and a father—not a star. He spends most of his free time with his family and has coached his son's little league team.

*Denzel and his family at a ribbon cutting ceremony at a Los Angeles hospital.*

Denzel also believes that it is very important to give back to the community. In the last few years, he has donated millions of dollars to many organizations, including his church, to a hospice for AIDS patients, and to South African President Nelson Mandela's Children Fund.

## Special Interests

- Denzel enjoys sports, especially skiing, running, weight lifting, and playing basketball, touch football, and tennis.
- Denzel likes to read, cook, and listen to music.

# Angela Bassett

> "It's in my background to persevere, you know. I'm a strong black woman. My mother is a strong black woman. So is my grandmother and my great-grandmother and my aunt. If nothing else ever happened, I know that I'd keep working. And if it all went away tomorrow, I know that I'd endure."

A ngela Bassett and her sister were raised by their mother in public housing in Florida. Angela first became interested in acting in 1974 when she went on a field trip to Washington, D.C. There she saw actor James Earl Jones in the play *Of Mice and Men*. She was very moved by his performance and "just sat there after the play, boo-hoo crying, weeping." She thought to herself, "If I could make somebody feel the way that I feel right now!" Then and there, she decided that she wanted to become an actor. She began appearing in church and school plays.

Because Angela was an excellent student, her mother encouraged her to go to college. After graduating from high school, she won a scholarship to Yale University in Connecticut. Angela knew that becoming an actor would be difficult, so she decided to study business. Later, with her mother's support, she changed her major to acting.

When Angela first arrived at college, she had a strong southern accent. As an actor, she had to learn to speak clearly and with different accents. She studied voice and acting with good instructors who recognized her rare talent. She spent six years at Yale, graduating with a Master's degree in drama.

After university, Angela got parts in television commercials, films, and the daytime soap opera *The Guiding Light*. She also began acting in plays. Angela's big break came with her role in John Singleton's 1991 film, *Boyz N the Hood*. She played the part of the strong mother of the young hero. Angela was inspired by her own mother's dedication to her two daughters.

In 1992, Angela acted in the film *Passion Fish*. She also appeared in Spike Lee's movie *Malcolm X*. Audiences were very impressed with her realistic portrayal of Betty Shabazz, the wife of civil rights activist Malcolm X. The same year, Angela also played the part of Michael Jackson's mother in a television miniseries about the family. Angela had to portray Katherine Jackson from the ages of fifteen to fifty-five.

## Personality Profile

**Career:** Actor.

**Born:** August 18, 1959, in New York City, New York.

**Education:** B.A., M.F.A., Yale University, 1982.

**Awards:** Golden Globe and Academy Award nomination for *What's Love Got to Do with It*.

Angela's first starring film role was as Tina Turner in *What's Love Got to Do with It*. Actor Lawrence Fishburne recommended Angela for the part. He agreed to act the role of Ike Turner only if Angela played Tina.

Playing Tina's life was very physically and emotionally difficult for Angela. To prepare for the role, she had a singing coach, a voice coach, and a personal trainer. She even broke her hand in one of the violent scenes in the film. Angela never complained. She had one very important fan—Tina Turner herself who came to watch her on the set. Angela was nominated for an Academy Award for best actress and won a Golden Globe Award for best actress for her performance.

Angela became a star after *What's Love Got to Do with It*. She suddenly found herself having to deal with fans stopping her in the streets. Despite this, she has remained down-to-earth and humble. She is known as a dedicated actor who insists on being treated fairly.

With her hard work, patience, and determination, Angela is finally getting the attention she deserves.

## Accomplishments

**1991** Appeared in *Boyz N the Hood*.

**1992** Appeared in two films, *Passion Fish*, and *Malcolm X*.

**1993** Starred as Tina Turner in *What's Love Got to Do with It*. Nominated for an Academy Award. Won a Golden Globe Award.

**1995** Appeared with Whitney Houston in the film *Waiting to Exhale*.

# Thelma "Butterfly" McQueen

T helma McQueen was an only child whose father left home when she was five. She spent her childhood moving from city to city while her mother searched for work. For a while, they settled in Harlem where her mother got a job as a cook.

After high school, Thelma took a course in nursing. However, she soon decided on a theatrical career and studied dance and acting. After her debut in the "Butterfly Ballet," she began to use "Butterfly" as her stage name.

*"I didn't mind playing a maid the first time, because I thought that was how you got into the business. But after I did the same thing over and over, I resented it. I didn't mind being funny, but I didn't like being stupid."*

**Career:** Actor.

**Born:** January 8, 1911, in Tampa, Florida.

**Died:** December 23, 1995, in Augusta, Georgia.

**Education:** B.A., City College of New York, 1975.

**Awards:** Black Filmmakers Hall of Fame Award, 1975; Emmy award for "The Seven Wishes of Joanna Peabody," 1979.

In the 1930s, Thelma began to get small parts in plays. Then she got the role of Prissy in *Gone with the Wind*. At first, Thelma was thrilled to get a role in such an important film. After reading the script, however, she was not so happy. Thelma fought for changes to her character. She thought that Prissy, a slave girl, was too stupid and lazy. Thelma refused to be filmed eating watermelon and spitting out the seeds because she thought this insulted African Americans.

Thelma was also unhappy about the way the black actors were treated during the filming of *Gone with the Wind*. She complained that the African-American actors had to use separate rest rooms from the white actors. While the white stars were driven around in limousines, the black actors had to share a crowded car. Thelma and the other African-American actors were not even allowed to attend the opening night of *Gone with the Wind* which was in a whites-only theater.

Despite all of her problems on the set of *Gone with the Wind*, Thelma was pleased with her work. Her high-pitched voice and talent for comedy pleased everyone who saw the film. Although the producers at first thought Thelma was too fat and old for the part, they later loved her as Prissy. The role also paid well and made her famous.

After *Gone with the Wind*, Thelma returned to the stage and appeared in several more films, nearly always as a maid. In the late 1940s, she refused to take any more parts playing maids and servants. Thelma paid a high price for this decision. She did not work in films for over twenty years.

To support herself during these hard years, Thelma acted in the theater whenever she could. She managed a theater group, taught at Southern Illinois University, ran a restaurant, and sold toys at Macy's department store. In 1951, with her own savings, she performed her own one-person show. Thelma played several small parts in films in the 1970s. In 1979, she won an Emmy award for her work in the children's television special "The Seven Wishes of Joanna Peabody."

Thelma was the guest of honor at the fiftieth anniversary celebration of the publication of the book *Gone with the Wind*. People began to remember her, and in the late 1980s, she was offered more film and television roles.

Although Thelma loved acting, community work was even more important to her. She taught at recreation centers and worked on environmental projects. She loved animals and campaigned for animal rights. In 1975, when she was sixty-four years old, she graduated from the City College of New York.

Thelma retired to a small cottage in Augusta, Georgia, where few people realized who she was. She died at the age of eighty-four in a house fire. She left her money to her friends and neighbors.

## Accomplishments

**1939** Appeared as Prissy in *Gone with the Wind*.

**1975** Graduated with a B.A. in political science from the City College of New York.

**1979** Won Emmy award for role in "The Seven Wishes of Joanna Peabody."

**1986** Appeared in *Mosquito Coast* with Harrison Ford.

# Will Smith

**W**ill Smith was the oldest of four children in a middle-class family in Philadelphia, Pennsylvania. As a child, Will always liked to perform and make people laugh. He was very bright but did not do well in school because he was always fooling around in class. In high school, he would disturb the class by making his friends laugh. His teachers called him Prince Charming because of his smooth excuses for not finishing assignments. With his mother's encouragement, Will studied harder and was accepted into engineering school in 1986. But his career was to take a different direction.

When he was twelve, Will had begun rapping for fun at parties. He soon became a successful rap artist, performing at local clubs. In 1986, Will started to work with another musician, Jeff Townes. They called themselves D.J. Jazzy Jeff and the Fresh Prince and put out an album called *Rock the House*, which sold over 500,000 copies. They released another album, *He's the D.J., I'm the Rapper*, which was even more successful. In 1988, D.J. Jazzy Jeff and the Fresh Prince won the first Grammy award for Best Rap Performance for the song "Parents Just Don't Understand." In 1991, they won another Grammy for the song "Summertime" from their fourth album, *Homebase*. That album went platinum. Before he was twenty years old, Will had gone on tour to London, Moscow, and Japan, and had become a millionaire.

Fame forced Will to learn some important lessons at a young age. Excited by his early success, Will spent money faster than he could earn it. He bought jewelry, a house, and six luxury cars. Will now says that "money disappears a lot faster than it comes in, no matter how much you make."

The head of the NBC television network saw Will perform and thought he would appeal to a younger audience. Will was offered his own series, "The Fresh Prince of Bel Air." He starred in the series from 1990 to 1996.

## Personality Profile

**Career:** Actor and rap artist.

**Born:** 1969 in Philadelphia, Pennsylvania, to Will and Caroline Smith.

**Education:** Graduated from high school in 1986.

**Awards:** Won Grammy for Best Rap Performance, 1988; Grammy for Best Rap Performance by a duo or group, 1991; honored at National Association for the Advancement of Colored People (NAACP) Image Awards as outstanding rap artist, 1992.

Will enjoyed his years on the show and believes he learned a lot there. When he was nominated for a Grammy in 1991, he promised the cast that he would take them to Hawaii if he won. After much teasing from the cast, he finally followed through with his promise. In 1994, he took nineteen people for four days to Maui.

In 1992, Will and his wife had a son. Will felt as if he had grown up instantly. As he said, "When the doctor handed him to me, I realized things were different now...being a dad changes everything."

In 1993, Will got a role in the movie *Six Degrees of Separation* where he played a con-artist. Will spent three hours a day for three months with speech and acting coaches to prepare for his role opposite experienced actors Stockard Channing and Donald Sutherland. In 1996, Will became one of the few African-American actors to star in a major action film. In *Independence Day*, Will was a pilot who helps save the world from aliens. For his next film, an action-comedy called *Men in Black*, Will will be paid $5 million, making him one of the highest paid African-American actors.

## Accomplishments

**1986** Put out *Rock the House* with D.J. Jazzy Jeff.

**1990-96** Starred in his own television series, "The Fresh Prince of Bel Air."

**1992** Appeared in *Made in America*.

**1993** Appeared in *Six Degrees of Separation*.

**1994** Starred in *Bad Boys*.

**1996** Starred in *Independence Day*.

# Mario Van Peebles

**M**ario Van Peebles had an unusual childhood. He is the eldest child of Melvin, an actor and director, and Maria, a professional photographer. He was born in Mexico and, as a child, lived in France, Morocco, and Denmark—wherever his parents went to work. His parents believed that travel would give their children a wider view of the world. The family often lived in hotels, and the children were educated by their mother.

After Mario's parents got a divorce, he and his sister Megan moved to San Francisco with their mother. Maria was an amazing person. Mario remembers hitchhiking with her to Altamont, California, where she got him drum lessons with the superstar rock group The Grateful Dead.

*"I want to go beyond racial lines and be just a filmmaker."*

Mario began acting when he was eleven years old. When he was fourteen, he appeared in a movie written and directed by his father, *Sweet Sweetback's Baadasssss Song*. Mario's father taught him that learning about the business side of the film industry was as important as learning how to act. He encouraged Mario to study economics at Columbia University in New York. After graduating, Mario worked for the New York City Department of Environmental Protection. After a year, he quit his job and asked his father to help him get work in the film industry. Melvin Van Peebles told his son to find his own work. Although Mario was disappointed at the time, he did just what his father advised.

## Personality Profile

**Career:** Actor, director, and writer.

**Born:** January 15, 1957, in Mexico City, Mexico, to Melvin and Maria Van Peebles.

**Education:** B.A., Columbia University, 1978.

At first, Mario got a few small stage roles and worked as a model and a photographer to make extra money. In the 1980s, Mario was given a part on the television soap opera "One Life to Live" and appeared on "The Cosby Show" and "L.A. Law." He also began to act in films, and in 1986, co-starred with Clint Eastwood in *Heartbreak Ridge*.

In 1987, Mario got his own television show, "Sonny Spoon," in which he played a street-smart private detective. Although the show lasted less than two years, it allowed Mario to try directing. He believes it is more interesting to control a film than it is to be in it.

Mario and his father have worked together several times. In 1988, they co-produced and acted in the film *Identity Crisis*. In 1990, they wrote a book about their experiences working together, *No Identity Crisis: A Father and Son's Own Story of Working Together*.

In 1991, Mario directed his first movie, *New Jack City*, which starred Wesley Snipes and the rapper Ice-T. Mario's business background was valuable. With careful planning, he made the movie in less time and with less money than was expected. *New Jack City* is about gangsters and crime and has a strong anti-drug and anti-violence theme. Critics were impressed with Mario's work, and the film did well.

Although the movie had an anti-violence message, riots broke out at several theaters where it was being shown. The problem was not the movie. It was theaters that had to turn away angry customers after overselling tickets.

One of the best moments of Mario's life happened during the screening of *New Jack City*. An African-American man stood up in the front row to yell, "Just say no, fool," as a character in the movie accepted some drugs.

## Accomplishments

**1971** Acted in *Sweet Sweetback's Baadasssss Song*.

**1987** Starred in the television series "Sonny Spoon."

**1991** Directed *New Jack City*.

**1993** Wrote, directed, and starred in *Posse*.

**1995** Directed and acted in *Panther*.

# Keenen Ivory Wayans

K eenen grew up in a family of ten children in Harlem, New York City. He was given his middle name, Ivory, after his grandfather. Keenen's parents were very strict, and the Wayans children were not allowed to play with the other kids in the neighborhood. They made their own fun telling jokes and imitating one another.

When he was six years old, Keenen saw Richard Pryor on television. Pryor's skit made Keenen laugh and reminded him about his own life. He realized how powerful comedy could be, and Pryor became his idol.

In high school, Keenen decided not to get involved with drugs. He was the class clown and loved to make his friends laugh. Although Keenen was bright, he had little time to study. He worked seventy hours a week as the manager of a fast food restaurant to help support his family. Even though his marks were not high, Keenen won a scholarship to study engineering at Tuskegee Institute in Alabama.

The summer after his first year of college, Keenen auditioned as a stand-up comic and was accepted. He realized then that he loved performing. He decided to leave school and become a professional comic in New York City.

In 1980, Keenen moved to Los Angeles, where he worked in comedy clubs and was a guest actor in many popular television series, including "Cheers," "Benson," and "A Different World." His big break came in 1982, when he was invited to appear on the "Tonight Show."

## Personality Profile

**Career:** Actor, comedian, screenwriter, filmmaker, and television producer.

**Born:** June 8, 1958, in New York City, New York, to Howell and Elvira Wayans.

**Education:** Seward Park High School; Tuskegee Institute.

**Awards:** Emmy award for best variety, musical, or comedy program for "In Living Color," 1990; Emmy nominations, 1990, 1991.

With his friend Robert Townsend, Keenen made a low-budget movie called *Hollywood Shuffle*. The film was a dark comedy that looked at the shortage of good film roles offered to African Americans. Keenen also co-wrote and co-produced *Eddie Murphy Raw*, which made more money than any other concert film in history.

Keenen wanted to make a film on his own, without the help of his friends. His 1988 film, *I'm Gonna Git You Sucka*, was a comedy-adventure in which blacks played both the heroes and the villains.

The Fox Television Network was impressed with Keenen's film and offered him the chance to produce his own television series. Keenen turned down the offer at first because he was not interested in television. He finally agreed when he was given complete control over the show. He became the executive producer and head writer of the "In Living Color" series which ran from 1990 to 1994. The cast of "In Living Color" included Keenen himself and his brother Damon and sister Kim, as well as comedian Jim Carrey.

"In Living Color" was very popular but was often criticized for being too outrageous or for going too far. In fact, Keenen's skits about Arsenio Hall harmed Keenen's and Arsenio's friendship.

Keenen has since signed a contract with CBS to produce other television programs.

## Accomplishments

**1982** Appeared on the "Tonight Show."

**1987** Made the film *Hollywood Shuffle* with Robert Townsend.

**1988** Wrote, directed, and starred in *I'm Gonna Git You Sucka.*

**1990** Produced the television series "In Living Color." Won an Emmy award for best variety, musical, or comedy program.

**1994** Wrote, directed, and starred in *A Low Down Dirty Shame.*

**1996** Starred in *The Glimmer Man.*

# Alfre Woodard

A lfre Woodard grew up in a loving and supportive family in Tulsa, Oklahoma. Her parents encouraged her to believe that she could do whatever she set her mind on doing. The Woodard children were aware of the world around them and were taught to care for other people. Every summer, the family took car trips to different parts of the United States so the children could learn how other people lived. Alfre's parents also insisted that their children watch television newscasts every day.

At the age of fourteen, Alfre showed an early talent for public speaking when she gave a speech to African-American business people. Her teachers encouraged her to act in the school play, and she also took drama classes. By the time she graduated from high school, she knew she wanted to be an actor.

*"I think that black actors like myself have altered Hollywood's narrow standards of beauty by not going away or even getting angry about it. We just had to be hired."*

Alfre majored in drama at Boston University in Massachusetts. In her theater courses, she studied plays and learned how to build sets as well as how to act. She performed in shows put on by the university's Black Drama Collective.

After graduating in 1974, Alfre did not get many acting jobs. She had moved to Los Angeles, but she worked as an actor for only three or four weeks a year. She was not even considered for most roles because of her dark skin and African-American look. Since Alfre had both self-confidence and the support of her family and friends, she was not discouraged by her slow climb to success. In the meantime, she joined an entertainment group, juggling, tap-dancing, and impersonating animals for children in schools. After much persistence, Alfre began to get parts in plays and small roles in motion pictures.

In 1983, Alfre appeared in the movie *Cross Creek*, in which she played a housekeeper. While the movie did not get many good reviews, Alfre was nominated for an Academy Award for best supporting actress. Alfre worked on several television series and was nominated for several Emmy awards. She won two, one for her appearances on "Hill Street Blues," and one for "L.A. Law." She has appeared in over a dozen feature films and as many made-for-television movies. Alfre can make the smallest role seem important. Today, she is one of the most highly respected performers in film and television.

## Personality Profile

**Career:** Actor.

**Born:** November 8, 1953, in Tulsa, Oklahoma, to Marion and Constance Woodard.

**Education:** B.A., Boston University, 1974.

**Awards:** Emmy awards, 1984 and 1987.

Alfre is aware of the problems black people face in many parts of the world. In the film *Mandela*, she played the part of Winnie Mandela, the wife of Nelson Mandela, because she wanted people to know about the problems blacks faced at the time in South Africa. Alfre helped start a group called Artists for a Free South Africa. In 1994, she went to South Africa to encourage blacks to vote in the first democratic election. She also belongs to the Hollywood Women's Political Committee.

Alfre is very choosy about her film roles and has turned down parts with which she was not comfortable. About new roles, she asks herself, "Is this something that my mother and father wouldn't be ashamed to watch?" For Alfre, "acting…is twenty-four hours a day of physically and emotionally being wrapped up with the character. So I can't bear doing things I don't like."

## Accomplishments

| | |
|---|---|
| **1979** Appeared in *Remember My Name*. | **1991** Appeared in *Grand Canyon*. |
| **1983** Nominated for best supporting actress Academy Award for her role in the film *Cross Creek*. | **1993** Starred in *Passion Fish*. |
| | **1994** Starred in Spike Lee's *Crooklyn*. |
| **1984** Won an Emmy award for her work on "Hill Street Blues." | **1995** Appeared in *How to Make an American Quilt*. |
| **1987** Won a second Emmy for her role on "L.A. Law" and an ACE award for her part in *Mandela*. | |

# Index

1 2 3 4 5 6 7 8 9 0 Printed in Canada 6 5 4 3 2 1 0 9 8 7